A Dorling Kindersley Book

Written by Mary Atkinson
Art Editor Mandy Earey
Deputy Managing Editor Dawn Sirett
Deputy Managing Art Editor
C. David Gillingwater
Production Josie Alabaster
Picture Research Jennifer Silkstone
and Angela Anderson

First published in Great Britain in 1997
by Dorling Kindersley Limited,
9 Henrietta Street, London WC2E 8PS

Visit us on the World Wide Web at http://www.dk.com

A CIP catalogue record for this book is available from the British Library.

ISBN 0-7513-5602-6

Colour reproduction by Chromagraphics, Singapore
Printed and bound in Italy by L.E.G.O.

The publisher would like to thank the following for their kind permission to reproduce their photograhs:

t=top, b=bottom, l=left, r=right, c=centre, BC=back cover, FC=front cover

Robert Harding Picture Library: endpapers, ASAP/AVI Hirschfield 10-11c, Peter Langone 14-15c, Mark Bolster 20bl; **The Image Bank**: Rob Van Petten 20-21c; **Photofusion**: Paul Baldesare 16tl; **Photographers Library**: 12-13c; **Tony Stone Images**: Tim Brown 6bl, Laurence Monneret FC c, 6-7c, Arthur Tilley 8tl, Chris Harvey 11br, Terry Vine BC c, 13br, Peter Cade 14tl, Graeme Harris 17br, Andy Sacks 18-19c, Jon Riley 21tr; **Telegraph Colour Library**: Antonio Mo 7tr, 8-9c, 16-17c, 19br; **Zefa**: 9br, 12tl, 18bl.

Additional photography by Jo Foord, Dave King, Liz McCaulay, Ray Moller, Susannah Price, Tim Ridley, Steve Shott, and Alex Wilson.

Contents

WHY is Mummy's tummy so big?

Questions children ask about the facts of life

Consultants: Diane Melvin, Clinical Child Psychologist, and Dr. Gwyneth Young, Paediatrician

DK

DORLING KINDERSLEY
London • New York • Stuttgart • Moscow • Sydney

Why is Mummy's tummy

Why don't daddies have babies?

Both a man and a woman are needed to make a baby, but a baby can only grow in a woman. A woman has ovaries that contain tiny human eggs, and she has a womb, a place where an egg can grow into a baby.

When a woman is going to have a baby soon, her tummy grows bigger and bigger. It stretches to make

getting so big?

room for the baby that's growing inside her. After nine months, the baby will be ready to be born.

Why is the baby in Mummy's tummy?
When a man and woman want a baby, they make love. Tiny seeds, called sperm, come out of the man's penis and go into the woman through a passage in her body called her vagina. When a sperm joins together with an egg, it grows into a baby inside the woman.

Why can't I

When you were a newborn baby, you knew little about what was going on. You didn't understand what you

Why do I have a birthday?
Your birthday is the day of the year on which you were born. It is the one day in each year that is special to you – it is the day you celebrate your birth. Every year, on that exact date, you become another year older. Do you know the date of your birthday?

remember being born?

were seeing and hearing, so you soon forgot about being born. Cuddles, sleep, and milk were more important to you.

Why was I born in a hospital?
Having a baby can be hard work. Many mothers go to a hospital where the nurses and doctors have special equipment to help with the birth. Other mothers choose to have their baby at home with help from a midwife.

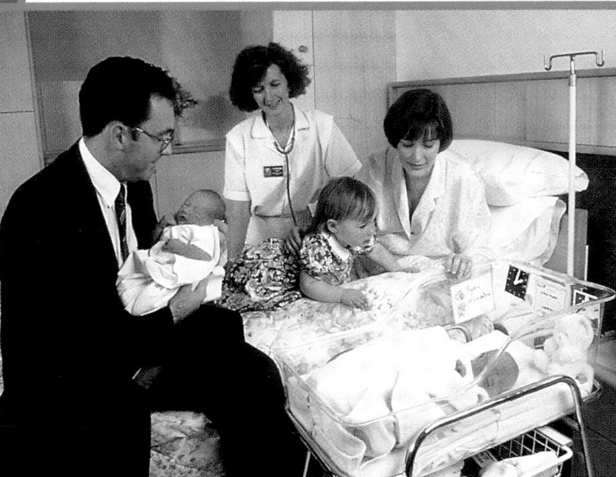

Why do babies

Young babies can't talk, and so they can't ask for what they want. One way they can get their mum and dad's attention is by crying. Whenever they're tired, hungry, uncomfortable, or needing a cuddle, they cry to let us know.

Why do babies sleep a lot?

Babies need more rest than children or adults because they're learning lots about the world and growing at a very fast rate. Newborn babies sleep almost all the time, although they wake regularly for a feed.

cry so much?

Why does Mum breast-feed the baby?

When a mother has a baby, milk is made inside her breasts. This milk is full of vitamins and energy to help her baby grow. The baby suckles the milk until it can eat solid food. Some babies drink special baby milk from a bottle instead.

Why do boys

Girls and boys have the different body parts they'll need to make a baby when they grow up. A boy has a

Why do I have a belly-button?
While you were in your mother's womb, a cord joined you to your mother. It went into your body at the place where your belly-button is now, and supplied you with food and oxygen. When you were born, the cord was cut off because you didn't need it anymore.

and girls look different?

penis and two testicles. A girl has a womb, a vagina, and two ovaries, which are all inside her body.

Why do we wear clothes even when it's hot? People feel that some parts of their bodies, such as the penis or vagina, are more private than other parts, so they cover them up when they're out. We don't have to let anyone else see or touch these parts.

Why do some children grow

We all grow up at our own pace. Some children have bigger bodies at younger ages than others; some want

Why do I have to grow up? Growing up and growing older are a part of life. Sometimes, we don't want things to change, but just as you wouldn't want to be a baby forever, once you're used to being an adult, you'll find that grown-up life can be fun, too.

up faster than others?

to do grown-up things before their friends. It doesn't matter how fast we grow up, as long as we enjoy being ourselves.

Why can't I have a baby?

Children's bodies are not ready to make babies. The body parts we need to make a baby don't usually finish growing until we're around twelve or thirteen years old. Even then, people wait until they're much older before deciding they're ready to look after a baby.

Why does my

When they're teenagers, many boys and girls feel attracted to one another and want to spend time

Why does my big sister have spots on her face?
Many teenagers have spots on their faces. They pop up because skin becomes oilier at this age. Most teenagers stop getting spots after a few years. In the meantime, eating healthy food and washing well can help clear up some spots.

big brother like girls?

together. They begin to feel these emotions at the same time as they start to develop grown-up bodies.

Why does my big sister want to be on her own?
Becoming an adult involves lots of changes that can be difficult until we get used to them. Teenagers often need time to themselves while they get used to their new grown-up bodies and feelings.

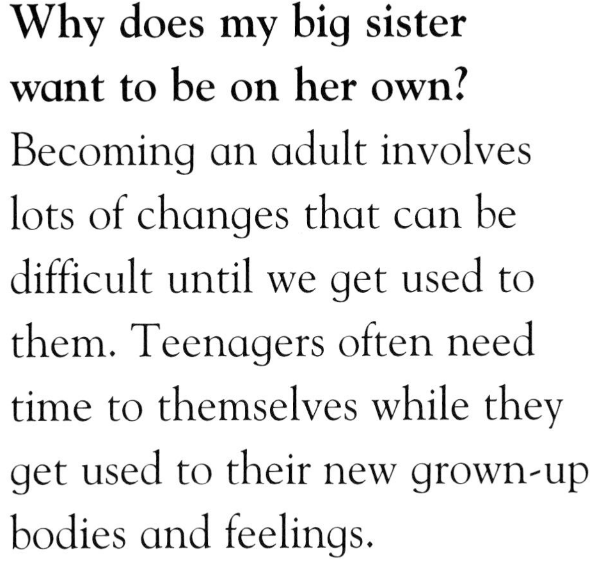

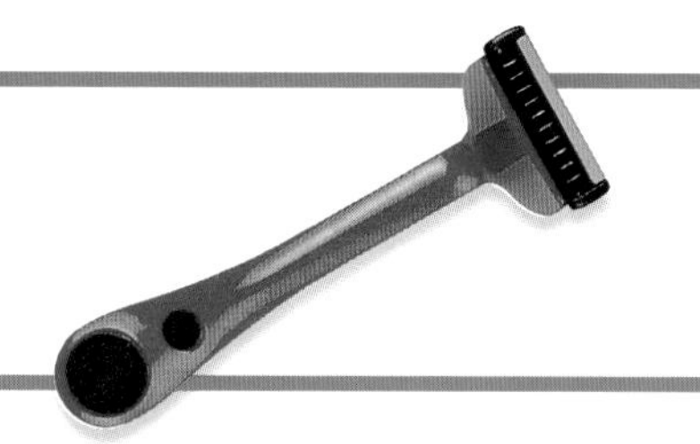

Why does Dad

As we grow into adults, our bodies change. One of the changes that happens as a boy grows into a man is that hair starts growing on his face. Shaving keeps his face smooth. If he wants a beard, he just stops shaving.

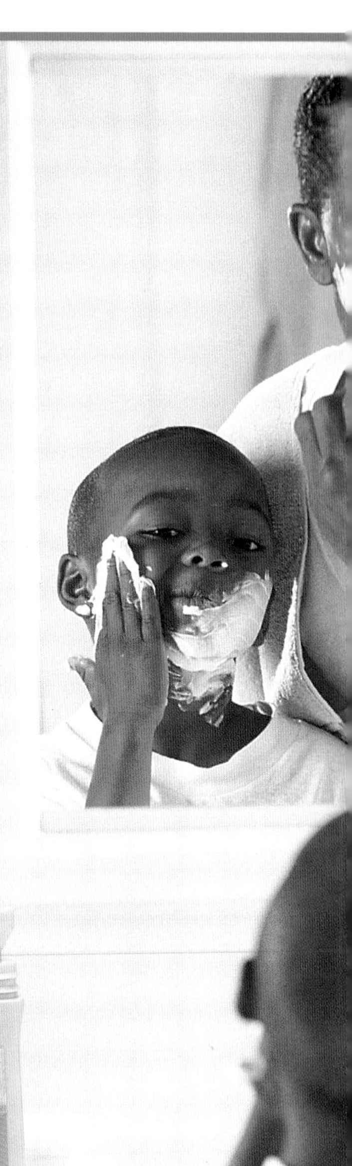

Why do grown-ups get so sweaty when they exercise? Sweating more, especially under the arms, is another of the changes that happens as we grow up. Many adults use deodorant under their arms to keep them dry and smelling fresh.

shave his face?

Why does Mum have breasts?
All girls grow breasts when they become women. This can happen at any age between around nine and fifteen years old. When a woman has a baby, her breasts produce milk for it to drink. Many women wear a bra to support their breasts and to keep them comfortable.

Why do grown-ups have such

Why do Mummy and Daddy sleep together?
Couples often sleep in the same bed. It's a private place where they can be close and make love. Snuggling up together every night is one way a couple can enjoy each other's company.

Part of being grown up is feeling attracted to other grown-ups. Long kisses make

long kisses?

a couple feel good, and are a way they can show their love for one another.

Why do so many grown-ups like love stories? Sharing their lives with the right partner is important to many grown-ups. That's why they enjoy hearing romantic stories about other couples who meet and fall in love – especially when the stories have happy endings.